Mules of Love

Mules
of Love

poems by
Ellen Bass

Introduction by Dorianne Laux

AMERICAN POETS CONTINUUM SERIES, NO. 73

BOA Editions, Ltd. 🌿 Rochester, NY 🌿 2002

10 11 12 6 5 4

For information about permission to reuse any material
from this book please contact The Permissions Company
at www.permissionscompany.com or email permdude@eclipse.net

Publications by BOA Editions, Ltd.—
a not-for-profit corporation under section 501 (c) (3)
of the United States Internal Revenue Code—
are made possible with the assistance of grants from
the Literature Program of the New York State Council on the Arts,
the Literature Program of the National Endowment for the Arts,
the Sonia Raiziss Giop Charitable Foundation,
the Lannan Foundation,
as well as from the Mary S. Mulligan Charitable Trust,
the County of Monroe, NY, Citibank,
and The CIRE Foundation.

See page 90 for special individual acknowledgments.

Cover Design: Daphne Poulin-Stofer
Interior Design and Typesetting: Richard Foerster
Manufacturing: McNaughton & Gunn, Lithographers
BOA Logo: Mirko

LIBRARY OF CONGRESS CATALOGING-IN-PUBLICATION DATA

Bass, Ellen.
    Mules of love : poems / by Ellen Bass.
        p. cm. — (American poets continuum series ; no. 73)
    ISBN 1-929918-22-4 (alk. paper)
    I. Title. II. American poets continuum series ; vol. 73.

PS 3552.A817 M87 2002
811'.54—dc21

2001056665

NYSCA

NATIONAL
ENDOWMENT
FOR THE ARTS

BOA Editions, Ltd.
Thom Ward, Editor/Production
Peter Conners, Editor/Marketing
Melissa Hall, Development Director/Office Manager
Bernadette Catalana, BOA Board Chair
A. Poulin, Jr., Founder (1938-1996)
250 North Goodman Street, Suite 306
Rochester, NY 14607
www.boaeditions.org

Contents

III. TULIP BLOSSOMS

IV. INSOMNIA

to Janet

Introduction

While with an eye made quiet by the power
of harmony, and the deep power of joy,
We see into the life of things.
—Wordsworth

Poet Ellen Bass sees into the life of things, creating a poetry that goes straight to the heart, in a voice that speaks to us clearly and intimately about the subjects of daily living: community, family, domestic life and sexual love. There are poems of political consciousness, personal, cultural, historical and environmental awareness, all of it handled with humor and grace. *Mules of Love* is luminous with the ordinary: an afternoon in the garden, a family car trip, a visionary moment on the front lawn with a neighbor, moments we are apt to miss the deeper significance of if we don't pay careful attention.

What is the poet's job but to help us to become aware of life's transience, love's power, the subtle manifestations of hope, to play for us again the ancient themes. When she speaks, her authority is clear, her wisdom and compassion evident. To her lover she offers her strength: "Bring me your pain, love. Spread / it out like fine rugs, / silk sashes, warm eggs, cinnamon / and cloves in burlap sacks. Show me...." She commiserates with the goddess Demeter: "In the story it sounds like sorrow's over. / They don't write how it never leaves, how it sounds in every / wind, in every rain, soaks / your heart like rain soaks the fields." In a poem to her daughter she recognizes the complicated weight of our love:

> You dug me out like a well. You lit
> the deadwood of my heart. You pinned me
> to the earth with the points of stars....
>
> Massive the burden this flesh
> must learn to bear, like mules of love.

Unafraid of the full range of human emotion, Bass also applies humor to the taboo subjects of sex, religion and death: "If this were the last / day of my life, I wouldn't / complain about the curtain rod..." and in "Birds Do It": "The young imagine lovers young, / sleek as tapers, waxy, gleaming. / And worry that their own lumpy legs, / pimples, hair thin as cilia—/ will shut them out, / tick them off the assembly line like seconds." In "God and the G-Spot," she positions herself firmly between the sacred and the profane: "Belief and disbelief / are a pair of tourists standing on swollen feet / in the Prado—*I don't like it. / I do.*—before the Picasso."

Bass is a poet of the elemental, always struggling to manage the science and biology of life with the mysteries of religion, philosophy and consciousness. It's as if she is so startled to be alive, she can't help asking every moment to stop and let her examine it, ask it a question. In "Insomnia" she finds herself awake while the world is at rest and commiserates with others afflicted with similar hungers.

> All over the world, people can't sleep.
> In different time zones, they are lying awake,
> bodies still, minds trudging along like child laborers.
>
> ...may something
> comfort you—a mockingbird, a breeze, the smell
> of crushed mint, Chopin's Nocturnes,
> your child's birth, a kiss,
> or even me—in my chilly kitchen
> with my coat over my nightgown—thinking of you.

Compassion and connection are among her gods, and so she exhorts the sleepless masses to seek the consolation of their own interwoven and quietly miraculous lives. In this age of violence and disconnection, as we spend more and more time looking for a technological fix, this kind of poetry is a necessary reminder to see our lives as a continuum of ordinary days, each bountiful, spacious, precious. Ellen Bass has created a woman who stands on the edge of her life, looking for the moment that might change us all.

—Dorianne Laux

I.
If There Is No God

Everything on the Menu

In a poem it doesn't matter
if the house is dirty. Dust
that claims the photographs like a smothering
love. Sand spilled from a boy's sneaker,
the faceted grains scattered on the emerald rug
like the stars and planets of a tiny
solar system. Monopoly
butted up against Dostoyevsky.
El techo, a shiny sticker, labeling the ceiling
from the summer a nephew studied Spanish.

Mold on bread in the refrigerator
is as interesting as lichen on an oak—
its minuscule hairs like the fuzz
on an infant's head, its delicate
blues and spring greens, its plethora of spores,
whole continents of creatures, dazzling our palms.

In a poem, life and death are equals.
We receive the child, crushed
like gravel under the tire.
And the grandfather at the open grave
holding her small blue sweatshirt to his face.
And we welcome the baby born
at daybreak, the mother naked, squatting
and pushing in front of the picture window
just as the garbage truck roars up
and men jump out, clanking
metal cans into its maw.

In a poem, we don't care if you got hired
or fired, lost or found love,
recovered or kept drinking.

You don't have to exercise
or forgive. We're hungry.
We'll take everything on the menu.

In poems joy and sorrow are mates.
They lie down together, their hands
all over each other, fingers
swollen in mouths,
nipples chafed to flame, their sexes
fitting seamlessly as day and night.
They arch over us, glistening and bucking,
the portals through which we enter our lives.

God and the G-Spot

He didn't want to believe. He wanted to know.
—Ann Druyan, Carl Sagan's wife,
on why he didn't believe in God

I want to know too. Belief and disbelief
are a pair of tourists standing on swollen feet
in the Prado—*I don't like it.*
I do.—before the Picasso.

Or the tattoo artist with a silver stud
in her full red executive lips,
who, as she inked in the indigo blue, said,
I think the G-spot's one of those myths
men use to make us feel inferior.

God, the G-spot, falling in love. The earth round
and spinning, the galaxies speeding
in the glib flow of the Hubble expansion.
I'm an East Coast Jew. We all have our opinions.

But it was in the cabin at La Selva Beach
where I gave her the thirty tiny red glass hearts
I'd taken back from my husband when I left.
He'd never believed in them. She, though, scooped
them up like water, let them drip through her fingers
like someone who has so much she can afford to waste.

That's the day she reached inside me
for something I didn't think I had.
And like pulling a fat shining trout from the river
she pulled the river out of me. That's
the way I want to know God.

If

It was in a house I'd never been to, a drug
I don't remember. His woman, my man—
and others—likewise occupied.
We'd come for that purpose. I took him
the way wind takes—
on its way someplace else.

Though we worked in the same South End brownstone
we'd never had a conversation. Nor did we then
when I eased down on him, slid
onto his stalk that was waiting
like a person for a bus.

When I heard he'd killed himself
of course I saw us, back then,
on the living room rug. I'm suspended
above him, propped on my gorgeous arms.
His eyes are the blue of oceans
with no land in sight.

What would have happened
if I'd gathered up the loose
pieces of him, like the change fallen
from our pockets, like the clothes
strewn around the room?

What would have happened if I'd
gathered those clothes
and held them up for him
as though he were weak from illness—
his shorts, first one leg
then the other; jeans,
step, step, as I would do later

with my own children, the T-shirt
guided down, head crowning.
Then each arm in a sleeve, their weight released,
they'd hang like the still warm bodies of game.
The socks I could have put on easily,
stretching each one and slipping it over the large
animals of his feet. Then zipping
the jacket closed like a scar.

Would it have changed anything
if I'd led him outside
and we'd walked through the city, gloved hands
in our pockets, and told each other everything—
the light snow falling, light
from the street lamps, the amber of weak tea,
the rose white of the sky?

Jack Gottlieb's in Love

I'm talking to Jack Gottlieb's son—my childhood
friend from Pleasantville. He was a skinny,
dark-haired guy, with a neck thin
as the stalk of a dahlia. We lived in railroad

apartments over our parents' stores—*Jack's Army & Navy,
Hy-Grade Wines & Liquors*. Now he's balding
and quadriplegic from the kiss
of an eight-axle truck. "My father's got a girlfriend,"

he tells me. "He's having more sex
than you and me and both our neighborhoods
combined." I picture Jack Gottlieb, eighty-six,
stroking the loosened skin of his beloved, puckered

as fruit left too long on the limb. Skin softened
the way I once read a pregnant woman—
stranded alone in a hut in Alaska—softened
a hide for her baby's birth, chewing it

hours and hours each day. Life has been gnawing
Jack Gottlieb like that. First his son, stricken,
stripped down to sheer being. His daughter dead
of brain cancer, and his wife following like earth
into that grave.

                              Comes love.
And all the cells in Jack's old organs stir.
The heart, which had been ready to kick back
and call it a day, signs on for another stint.

The blood careens through the crusted arteries
like a teenage skateboarder. He kisses

each separate knob of her spine, the shallow basin
of her belly, her balding pudendum—crowning it

like a queen. The sad knave that's hung
between his legs, extraneous and out-of-date,
ill-fitting as his old vest, is now steam
pressed and ready for the ball.

                        Comes love.
Jack Gottlieb enters her over and over.
He's a child sledding down a hill and climbing
up again, face flushed, hot breath

visible in the twilight. He can't believe
her goodness. Life, that desperate addict,
has mugged and robbed him on the street,
and then she appears, taking his head

in her palms. He handles her reverently,
as though she were the Rosetta stone, revealing
what lies beyond hope. He scoops her into his hands
and she pours through his fingers again and again.

Remodeling the Bathroom

If this were the last
day of my life, I wouldn't complain
about the shower curtain rod
in the wrong place, even though
it's drilled into the tiles.
Nor would I fret
over water marks on the apricot
satin finish paint, half sick
that I should have used semigloss. No.
I'd stand in the doorway
watching sun glint
off the chrome faucet, breathing in
the silicone smell. I'd wonder
at the plumber, as he adjusted the hot
and cold water knobs. I'd stare
at the creases behind his ears and the gray
flecks in his stubble. I'd have to hold
myself back from touching him. Or maybe
I wouldn't. Maybe I'd stroke
his cheek and study
his eyes the amber of cellos, his rumpled
brow, the tiny garnet
threads of capillaries, his lips
resting together, quiet as old friends—
I'd gaze at him
as though his were the first
face I'd ever seen.

His Teeth

We haven't had rain
so I'm out here, thumb against the mouth
of the hose, spraying full force
and fretting that I've botched the roses—
when he crosses the lawn
in his terrycloth robe, leans
against the car, and cries.
I start toward the faucet,
but *no*, he says, *keep on.*
So I stand there, stream trained
on the crew cuts of the ornamental grasses
while he tells me he got gonorrhea
from his partner's twenty minute suck-off
with a guy in a car on West Cliff.
Using nicer words. This is a man
who walks me home at night
though it's only next door.
I stroke his back. The hardness
surprises me. It's muscled as a tree.
He stands barefoot on the cold cement,
one foot lapped up on the other.
Tears pool in the shallows
under his eyes which are pale blue
and, I realize, too far apart.
As sun tops the cedars and hits
him full face, he doesn't raise a hand
against it, just goes on, *I thought we were...*
I watch his mouth as he speaks, his chapped lips,
the sheen of pale stubble. But mostly
his teeth—they shine in the light,
slightly yellow, intricately striated,
tiny vertical fissures like the crazed
enamel of an old vase,

like stress lines in ice.
I can't take my eyes off his teeth—
and inside, the wet pink gums,
glistening, and so vulnerable
like something being born
right there, on the street,
with cars going by.

In Which a Deer Is Found in a Bubble Bath, Having Entered the House, Turned on the Faucet, Knocked Over the Bottle, and Stepped In— Not Necessarily in That Order

from an account in The Santa Cruz Sentinel

Did he hear splashing
as he tossed his keys
on the counter, or was the deer

composed by then, on all fours, suds
swirling around its delicate
ankles like a person standing

in shallow surf? Or did it lower
itself like a sphinx, the line
of wet fur dark around its neck

trimmed with an Elizabethan
collar of foam? Perhaps,
when it felt the water

warm as sunshine, smelled the rose
scented froth, it leaned back,
resting the separate knobs

of its vertebrae on the plump
plastic cushion, relaxing
like a woman after a long

shift at work.
If so, did the man know
what to do? Did he pour two

gin and tonics, carry them
on the silver tray his mother
left him, along with a stack

of ecru towels, then sit
on the lid of the toilet
and ask about her day?

Pay for It

Choose what you want and then pay for it.
—Robert Bly

I've chosen. There's no
doubt about it. I'm rooted
in this coastal town
where spring begins in January,
acacias bursting into chrome yellow
clusters, spiking the air with their
sharp scent. I am here
with my hands in the dirt,
yanking out crab grass,
planting a lemon tree.

You are shoveling snow—
or I picture you that way. Maybe
you have paid a boy to do it
and are walking through the cleared
path to your car. No. The car
is in the garage. This shows
how little I really know.

Do you remember those mornings—scraping ice
off the windshield, the car so frigid.
And the time you plowed into a snowbank just
as you hit the high notes
of "On the Street Where You Live."
I could have abandoned the car,
checked into the motel at the ramp's end
and never left. Or stayed right there,
frozen gladly, my mouth
fused to yours, an ice sculpture.

I do know in the evenings you make a fire.
You wrote that in a letter.
We make fires too when the nights get cold.
Well, not *cold*, of course, but my boy
likes a fire. And Janet.
They poke the logs, watching embers
spray, lit fountains in the night.

And you are reading. Your wife,
on the couch beside you,
reads a line aloud from *Middlemarch*.
Soon you'll place bookmarks and
go upstairs. I've seen your room
with its sloping ceiling. Your bed.
I won't imagine more.

Soon I will read to my child,
rub my face in the warm curve of his neck.
Janet's dragged the garbage to the curb
and calls me out to the crescent moon.
I can see it from the window,
thin as frost. When I go to her
we will lean together like horses.
I have made my choice. Still

there are mornings when I wake, my lips
swollen from your kisses,
my body bruised and fragrant
as grasses on which lions have lain,
and for a full bereft moment, I cannot,
for the life of me, remember
why I left.

Sometimes, After Making Love

When we feel the blood slip
through our arteries and veins,
sliding through the capillaries, thin as
root hairs, bringing bliss to the most
remote outposts of our bodies, delivering
oxygen and proteins, minerals, all the rich
chemicals our cells crave and devour
as we have devoured each other, I
lie there as sound reasserts itself,
and listen to the soft ticking of the clock
and a foghorn, faint from the lighthouse;
a car door slams across the street,
and I want to say something to you,
but it's like trying to tell a dream,
when the words come out flat as
handkerchiefs under the iron and the listener
smiles pleasantly like a person who doesn't
speak the language and nods at everything.
It should be enough that we have
lived these hours, breathing
each other's breath, catching the wind
in the sails of our bodies.
It should be enough. And yet
I carry the need for speech, strung
on the filaments of my DNA like black pearls,
from the earliest times when our ancestors
must have lain still, in amazement,
and groped for the first words.

If There Is No God

Then there's no one
to love us indiscriminately,
to twirl our planet like a globe, to keep the sap—
xylem and phloem—gliding up and down like the slide
of a trombone, the cells breathing through teeming mitochondria,
slurping rain, eating sunlight.

The jawless lamprey clamps its round
mouth on the flank of a fish, rasping and sucking blood.
The hinged-jaw python ingests a velvet-cloaked gazelle.

Spider silk, the polypeptide chain folded
back and forth, pleated sheets stronger than steel.
They stretch and coil, responding like a lover.
Who will notice? Who will watch
while the articulate legs wrap the dragonfly
round and round, huge wings whirring?

Who will crouch beside the lichen as it wheedles into rock,
mark its single millimeter's growth like a father penciling tracks
up the back of the door? And when it dies—
a thousand, two thousand years old, this modest
leaflike, shrublike creature, poisoned,
who will mourn? Who will chant its elegy?

The polar ice caps are cracking up.
The people of whole continents collapsing—viruses bud
continuously from the graceful, convoluted surfaces of T cells,
gathering and heaping in intricate curls and valleys.
We cannot find a single ivory-billed woodpecker or Tasmanian wolf.
Radioactive fallout circles the planet.

There must be something you love: the cherry trees
on Storrow Drive bursting into bloom as you pass,
each tree releasing its pale buds like pastel fireworks.
Or driving back from Poipu Beach, the children slumped against you,
the moon flashing through the thousand palms.

When finches go crazy gorging and singing
in the last of the November pears, when Pavarotti sings,
or a mother sings to her baby, "I can't give you anything but love,"
walking the stained carpet of the hallway,
when she falls back into bed and her new lover gathers
her up like honeycomb, someone
must pay attention. Open your window.
Listen, listen to them, and behold.

II.
Birds Do It

Birds Do It

The young imagine lovers young,
sleek as tapers, waxy, gleaming.
And worry that their own lumpy legs,
pimples, hair thin as cilia—
will shut them out,
tick them off the assembly line like seconds.
But even all those ads that tuck in
foil packets of scented cream
can't stop the fat woman with the bad perm
who serves cold croissants at the airport,
the bus driver mumbling through ill-fitting teeth,
the grocery clerk with tufts of hair sprouting from his ears—
they all just made love. Or are about to.
See the two stocky women at the Christmas party
who apologize for leaving early.
The one with the candy cane earrings
and Santa Claus pin on her scarf
takes the arm of the one in the green polo shirt
as they stand in the doorway, smiling
as if for a prom picture. It won't be long
before they reach into each other
like those Filipino healers, their hands
parting flesh as though the body
were not a solid thing, but mass
truly energy, the hot atoms
opening like the red sea,
until all that's left of them is steam.

Backdoor Karaoke

At The Backdoor Karaoke a man
I would not recognize again
sang "I Love You For Sentimental Reasons"
to his fiancée. Clean shaven, a little overweight—
not the kind of guy who bends over, showing his crack,
but one who could be handy with the remote—
he looked down at the monitor and gave it his best.
And as I twirled the ice in my second
Johnnie Walker Black—working up to my own
"Embraceable You"—I thought again how
astonishing that we pick someone out of the
countless people who stream by like schools
of silver anchovies. We pair up
to practice loving, the way we once
practiced kissing on the cold glassy
surface of the mirror or the mute
backs of our hands. We try to be kind.
We get used to their quirks,
grinding teeth in sleep, farting in the morning.
We find what to treasure—the way she reads aloud,
her cry at the crest of sex, his hand
dry and quiet as cloth at the funeral of a child.
And we give what we can—willingness
to get out of bed and look for the cat,
forgiveness for an old affair, a real attempt
not to always be right. We act as though
it's natural as geese mating for life,
but I cannot get over my wonder
that you come home day after day and offer
yourself, casually as the evening paper.

Poem to My Sex at Fifty-One

When I wash myself in the shower
and afterward, as I am drying
with the terrycloth towel,
I love the feel
of my vulva, the plump outer lips
and the neat inner ones
that fit together trimly
as hands in prayer. I like
to feel the slick crevice and the slight
swelling that begins
with just this casual handling.
So eager, willing as a puppy.
When I was young I could
not have imagined this
as I looked at women like me,
my waist thickened like pudding,
my rear end that once rode high
as a kite, now hanging like a
sweater left out in the rain,
skin drooping, not just the dewlaps
or pennants that flutter
under the arms, but all over,
loosening from the bone like boiled
chicken. And it will only
get worse. But that fleshy
plum is always cheerful. And new.
A taut globe shining
in an old fruit tree.

Basket of Figs

Bring me your pain, love. Spread
it out like fine rugs, silk sashes,
warm eggs, cinnamon
and cloves in burlap sacks. Show me

the detail, the intricate embroidery
on the collar, tiny shell buttons,
the hem stitched the way you were taught,
pricking just a thread, almost invisible.

Unclasp it like jewels, the gold
still hot from your body. Empty
your basket of figs. Spill your wine.

That hard nugget of pain, I would suck it,
cradling it on my tongue like the slick
seed of pomegranate. I would lift it

tenderly, as a great animal might
carry a small one in the private
cave of the mouth.

Marriage Without Sex

I don't know how people stay married
without sex. How they can stand their mates
day in, day out, the irritations grating
like sand under the band of your bathing suit
when you're sunburned and greasy and one kid
doesn't want to leave and the other one's crabbing,
there's no more juice and too much to carry to the car.
How could they tolerate it
week after week—the way he does the laundry,
mixing darks and lights, how he dangles
spaghetti from his mouth and chomps
along the strands like a cow, or when she
repeats what she read in the paper, as though
she thought of it herself, doesn't answer
when he speaks, or gets lost
going someplace she's been twenty times before.
How can couples bear
each other without the glory
of their bodies rising up like whales, breaking
the surface in a glossy arc,
finding each other in the long smooth flanks,
hidden coves, the gift of sound rushing
from their throats like spray.
What could make them appreciate
each other enough to stay without
this ocean that smooths the crumpled beach,
leveling the ground again.

Sleeping With You

Is there anything more wonderful?
After we have floundered
through our separate pain

we come to this. I bind myself to you,
like otters wrapped in kelp, so the current
will not steal us as we sleep.

Through the night we turn together,
rocked in the shallow surf,
pebbles polished by the sea.

The Sad Truth

My lover is a woman. I cherish
her sex—the puffy lips of the vulva
like ripe apricot halves, the thin inner lips
that lie closed, gently as eyelids.
I love the slippery slide up her
vagina and the whole thing thrown open
like a Casa Blanca lily. I savor her
taste and smell and how easily she can
pop out one lovely orgasm after another
like a baker turning out loaves of fragrant bread.
Sixteen years and I haven't grown tired
of that oasis, that mouth watering hole.
Yet sometimes, I do miss a penis,
that nice thick flesh that hardens
to just the right consistency. I miss
feeling it nudge me from behind in the night,
poking in between my legs. And the way it goes
out ahead, an envoy, blatant and exposed
on the open plain. It's so easy
to get its attention.
It jumps up in greeting like a setter.
And I'd enjoy it stuffed inside me
like a big wad of money in a purse.
I don't want another lover, but
sometimes I recall it. That longing
grabs me by the waist, dips me back,
sweeps my hair across the polished floor.

Tigers and People

On the eve of our seventeenth anniversary
Janet and I are arguing about whether to take a morning
walk. It reminds me way too much of my first marriage
and I'm about to tell her so when our son asks for help
with the tiger report he's mad he has to write
in the voice of a tiger because his science teacher
had a nervous breakdown and the substitute
used to teach English. He got a haircut today,
the sideburns sliced off high and sharp, angled
above the pale blue shadow of his exposed skin.
I read the screen over his shoulder:
My habitat is being destroyed at a rate of 50 acres a minute.
"What do you think I should say next?" he asks.

We've just returned from a week with my mother
so she's fed up with me to start with. I'm fed up
with myself. I rearranged the turkey sandwiches
for the flight home because she'd thrown them,
haphazardly, in the plastic bag.
Now, I hear her running a bath
for a little relief. Her hormones are fleeing.
She's only got a spritz of estrogen left,
like the last sputter of windshield wiper fluid.

I sit on the lid of the toilet seat. She says she's sorry,
that she'd love to take a walk with me. And when she sinks
in the shallow water, her breasts
fall back into her body as though they've given up.
I start to cry. The next morning
we'll fight again. And then we'll make up.
And over the years that follow we'll continue
to irritate and disappoint each other. And our son
will write many more reports—stupid and not.

And we'll eat more turkey sandwiches and visit our mothers
until they die and we wish they were still alive
to fuss that we didn't put the bagels, before they got moldy,
back in the refrigerator. The only thing that won't turn out
reasonably all right will be the tigers.

On Seeing Bernini's Ecstasy of Saint Teresa

When I stared at her face, slack
with lack of will, her mouth
open as a deep pool, so exposed,
I could almost watch
the breath rush in,

and the angel, gazing down
as though he'd created her,
scooped her from the rough rock
like a drowning woman from the sea,
smoothed her gleaming face, her supple
hand, carved the whipped
waves of her gown,

when I looked up, deep gold spikes
shooting from the sky: Teresa,
drenched in rapture, the angel glistening
with delight—

I thought of you last Sunday morning
standing over me in your leopard bra from Ross.

You had the same infinitely tender smile
and the same burning arrow in your hand.

Can't Get Over Her

My nephew is distressed that he's still
in love with the girl who went back to her boyfriend—
the one who's not good enough for her.

When he ran into her again, she had that same bright laugh,
like the shine on an apple, and the wind rose
reaching up into the limbs and fluttering
the leaves in the whole apple tree.

But when she left, it hit him all over.
She was headed for her boyfriend's house, she'd walk
quickly in the brittle March night.
He'd have a fire going. She'd unlace her boots
and offer him her mouth, her lips still cold,
velvet tongue warm in that satin cape.

He didn't tell me all this,
of course, but who hasn't longed
for that girl? that boy? He's mad
at himself that he can't get over her.

He's young and he's got goals, quit
smoking, gave up weekend drunks. Now he tackles
model airplane kits, one small piece at a time.
He wants to learn mastery. Sweet man.
Should we tell him the truth?

That he'll never get over her. Love
is a rock in the surf off the Pacific. Life
batters it. No matter how small it gets
it will always be there—grain of sand
chafing the heart. I still love

the boy who jockeyed cars, expertly
in the lots on New York Avenue,
parking them so close, he had to lift his lithe body
out the window those sultry August afternoons.
He smelled of something musky and rich—distinctive
as redwoods in heat.

I still long for him
like a patriot exiled from the motherland,
a newborn switched in the hospital, raised
in the wrong family. Each year that passes
is one more I miss out on. His children
are not mine. Even their new
stepmother is not me. When she complains

how hard she tries, how little they appreciate it,
I think how much better off he'd be with me.
And when he has grandchildren
they won't be mine either. And when he's dying—
even if I go to him—I'll be little more
than a dumb bouquet, spilling my scent.

We don't get over any of it. The heart
is stubborn and indefatigable. And limitless.
That's how I can turn to my beloved, now,
with the awe the early rabbis must have felt
opening the Torah. And when she pulls me to her,
still, after all these years, I feel like I did
the first time I stood in front of *Starry Night*.

I had never known, never imagined
its life beyond the flat, smooth surface
of the textbook. Had never conceived
there could be these thick swirls of paint,
the rough-edged cobalt sky, the deep
spiraling valleys of starlight.

III.
Tulip Blossoms

For My Daughter on Her Twenty-First Birthday

When they laid you in the crook
of my arms like a bouquet and I looked
into your eyes, dark bits of evening sky,
I thought, *of course this is you,*
like a person who has never seen the sea
can recognize it instantly.

They pulled you from me like a cork
and all the love flowed out. I adored you
with the squandering passion of spring
that shoots green from every pore.

You dug me out like a well. You lit
the deadwood of my heart. You pinned me
to the earth with the points of stars.

I was sure that kind of love would be
enough. I thought I was your mother.
How could I have known that over and over
you would crack the sky like lightning,
illuminating all my fears, my weaknesses, my sins.

Massive the burden this flesh
must learn to bear, like mules of love.

Working in the Garden

When jasmine sprawls over the fence, seductive
as a languid woman, I am pleased.
And when narcissi send up slender stalks,
but no luscious flowers, I'm disappointed.
But if one fails, the other thrives. Nature
is like that. It doesn't care. This seed
lands in fertile soil, the sun, the rain is right.
It grows to a sapling, then madrone,
limbs bronzed as children by the sea all summer.
That another lands on rock or is washed away
or sprouts and is trampled, doesn't matter.
Nature wants life, but any life will do.
I stay outside till dark, hashing up the ground.
Inside is my daughter. She has split
the hard shell of her seed
and a lone naked root is searching the soil.
I don't even know what she needs.
Anything I offer—or withhold—
may be wrong. And she can't tell me.
She is mute as a plant. And so individual,
like the bean I grew in a jar in third grade,
my own bean, the tiny white hairs of its root
delicate as the fuzz on a newborn's crown.
Just a singular seed and the treacherous odds.

Oh Demeter

In the story it sounds like sorrow's over.
They don't write how it never
leaves, how it sounds in every
wind, in every rain, soaks
your heart like rain soaks the fields.

Even at the very beginning of spring
when the whole luscious season stretches
before you, when wildflowers bloom from every
crevice of the gray stone cliffs, never
does a moment pass when your heart
is not anchored by the knowledge
that Persephone must leave.

A deal was made. One third
for Hades, two thirds for you:
the original custody suit.
And though you were a goddess,
though you could strike
and not a sprout of grain, not a grape,
not an olive would grow, still
you couldn't shift the balance any further.
And neither can I.

Gladly I would have stopped the poppies
from waving their brilliant flares, frozen
the stiff curled leaves of kale, twining peas,
and left them to blacken.

What the story doesn't tell is how you go on,
year after immortal year. How even in the thick
heat of summer, when bees swarm in the broad leaves
and figs swell like aroused women, even then

sorrow coats you like salt,
a white residue on the rich black furrows.

And life will never be the same. Even
when you get her back. Hell leaves its mark.

Your heart, like mine, is shattered, an ancient urn.
I have pieced the shards together,
but much is dust. Even in summer
wind blows through the cracks.

They begged you to allow the corn to grow again.
They write that you were kind
but I think kindness had little to do with it.
You'd done what you could.
People may as well eat.

Worry

"You always think the worst
is going to happen," Janet says
as we walk with our son along the Amsterdam canals.
"What do you think—he's going to fall in and drown?"

I have worried
all over the world. It comes to me easily.
Formed slowly through childhood
like stalactites in a cave.

My mother worried to keep going—
a sick husband, the store, children
she wanted everything for. I call her
distraught. Janet's been dizzy for days.
In the E.R. they inked small x's
on the parchment map of her skin.
Her doctor's at a conference in Paris,
and I'm afraid there's a blood clot near her brain.
"Go buy a plant," she says. "I'm not going to die."

My mother tells me I learned it from her—
how to panic. She was thirteen,
oldest of five, when her father left.
My grandmother worried to keep food
on the table. Every week
she'd board the bus to buy
dry goods, children's clothes, socks
to sell in her corner store.
When she didn't climb down
from the six o'clock—winter,
it was already dark—my mother sat
in the window, tears rumpling her face,
praying, *Let her come home.*

And in Russia—my father was a baby
when his mother carried him and two brothers
to the border. Hiding
in the forest undergrowth, my father
crying, she heard boots
bite through the crusted snow. Some women
smothered infants. What must have gone
through her mind when the steps hesitated,
before turning away?

Janet doesn't think about what
might happen. She thinks about what is.
But I carry dread on my shoulders
like a knapsack, like the extra pounds
my grandmother wanted me to gain.
She'd read about a girl in a plane crash.
All she had to eat was snow.

In My Hands

for my son

It was late November, a handful of stars,
chips of ice flung across the black sky.
And the moon, a smudge, rimmed
with a rib of frost.

We'd been in the hot springs
and I was dressing in the thick dark.
He'd been bundled in a sweater, boots,
knitted cap. Then—*What's that?*—
his sister's voice slit the night.

I have never been fast, or good
in a crisis. But this one time
I leapt toward that faintest of sounds,
a splash no louder than a bird might make
ruffling the water with its wing.

I slid into the pool, precise
as a knife. And as I reached down,
he was there, woolen arms
extended, reaching up.

I'd grabbed for the moon
and held it in my
hands, steaming, luminescent,
impossibly bright.

Guilt

At my child's school the teacher asks,
"Who knows what Yom Kippur is?"
A girl in red barrettes waves her hand.
"It's a time," she says brightly, "when you think
about what you're sorry for."
She is eight and her bowl of sins
seems empty as a dish the cat's licked clean.

But I am sorry for it all. Sorrow
grows in me like cattails choking
a pond. Sorrow, regret, remorse.

I never understood why people didn't want
children. They seemed tight-hearted,
intent on keeping cracker crumbs from littering
their Berber carpets. How could they give up
the hyacinth kisses, the heads soft as lambs' ears?
Maybe they already knew
when you have a child you sign up
for a love that can carve
a canyon in your heart.

I made mistakes. Hopeful, earnest,
cowardly mistakes. Big ones
from which little ones stemmed,
branching off into the future.

I think of Otto Frank, when he finally went for tickets
there were no tickets.
Two years of hiding, so calm, so dignified, so just.
The hero of his daughter,
voice of reason in the Annex.

If you could tell right from wrong,
it wouldn't be so hard to choose.

And the idea that God forgives our sins
is attractive, but I believe we drag them along.
Fasting, prayer, good works,
there is no erasing.

It's like building up layers
in a painting, one wash of color glazed
over another. Cumulative. Indelible.

Laundry

This morning my son left two wet footprints
on the bathmat, dark and flat
in the green fluff, one with a scrap
of brown bag pressed into it
like a bit of petal.

And I thought how, if anything
happened to him, that imprint
would remain, briefly,
shimmering in the shock
that aims a spotlight on the details of our world.

Folding laundry after your accident,
I sat on the floor by the basket of tousled clothes—
they had been washed and dried
while you were still unbroken—
and smoothed your empty shirts against my chest.

Happiness After Sorrow

No days were good, but some were worse.
I'd gotten as far as my door—reach out,
they always tell you—then had to pee.
Two steps toward the bathroom. But
what did peeing matter? I slid down
like a coat shrugged off. And slumped there,
on the edge of the frayed rug, I catalogued the worst
things that could happen to a parent. This—
my daughter stripping the medicine chest, rimming
the sink with plastic cylinders, her life
suspended in transparent amber—
was number three.

And then years pass. And you're making meatballs.
Exactly the way your family likes them.
A little bread crumbs. A little matzoh meal.
No egg. A dash of sherry.
You're browning them in the pan. Diana Krall's
singing "Peel Me a Grape." And you're happy.
The present is what you're crazy for,
each moment plump and separate as a raindrop
reflecting the world on its curved skin.

It happens. Our troubles familiar
as the peeling paint in the back
hallway, the stain on the couch
where the cat threw up.
We live with all the unbearable knowledge—
the hole in the ozone, the H-bomb,
and right now fathers are hurrying
children in their arms across barbed-wire borders.
After we weep, we fold the newspaper
and drive our kids to school.

How do we do it? How do we want
to make supper again? Squeezing
cold mush through my fingers, patting
it into pies. How does the love keep
swelling in the cavities of our frail bodies,
how do these husks hold so much jagged
pleasure in their parched split skins?

I tip the pot, oily water rushes out
and steam rises. All I have lost
swirls around me. I scoop
the mist with my palms.

The Moon

Driving south on highway one, along the crumbling
edge of the continent, I see it, the moon,
framed in the windshield like a small white shell

glued to the blue silk of the afternoon. Except it isn't.
It's the moon. All 1.62×10^{23} pounds of it, suspended,
with its mountains and maria, its craters, ridges and rilles.

"Isn't it amazing," I say to my lover and my son,
"to think the moon is really there and we can see it?"
She shrugs, cracking a salted sunflower seed.

Wires from a portable CD player pour Third Eye Blind
into my son's perfectly shaped ears. So I am alone
with my epiphany and the moon,

that I have come, just now, to realize is truly out there—
not a silver coin, a saucer of milk,
a creamy mound rising over the horizon of a tight bodice,

not an onion in the martini sky, not the surprised
mouth of heaven, or the whole round face of God,
this moon is the moon,

circling in its own private orbit of slight eccentricity,
so close I can make out the smooth shadow of the Sea of Rains
and trace the rough, bright peaks of the ranges.

After Our Daughter's Wedding

While the remnants of cake
and half-empty champagne glasses
lay on the lawn like sunbathers lingering
in the slanting light, we left the house guests
and drove to Antonelli's pond.
On a log by the bank I sat in my flowered dress and cried.
A lone fisherman drifted by, casting his ribbon of light.
"Do you feel like you've given her away?" you asked.
But no, it was that she made it
to here, that she didn't
drown in a well or die
of pneumonia or take the pills.
She wasn't crushed
under the mammoth wheels of a semi
on highway 17, wasn't found
lying in the alley
that night after rehearsal
when I got the time wrong.
It's animal. The egg
not eaten by a weasel. Turtles
crossing the beach, exposed
in the moonlight. And *we*
have so few to start with.
And that long gestation—
like carrying your soul out in front of you.
All those years of feeding
and watching. The vulnerable hollow
at the back of the neck. Never knowing
what could pick them off—a seagull
swooping down for a clam.
Our most basic imperative:

for them to survive.
And there's never been a moment
we could count on it.

Tulip Blossoms

Tulip trees hang over the Kalihiwai River,
large lemon-yellow flowers dangling from both banks.
As my son and I glide in a rented kayak,
they fall to the celadon surface, floating
like blessings in a private ritual.
When I smooth one open, the flat crepe petals
fan out, revealing a center so red
it's almost black—redder
than blood, or port,
or the deepest bing cherries—hidden
in the core of the blossom, the rippled base.
"It looks like an asshole,"
my son observes softly, almost
to himself. And I am glad,
remembering the first time
I saw his dusky asterisk,
its perfect creased rays—
glad he can see the flower
in the most humble, darkest star.

IV.
Insomnia

Mighty Strong Poems

for Billy Collins

"What mighty strong poems," he said.
And I repeat it all day, staggering
under sheaves of rejections.
But my poems, oh yes, they are brawny.
Even now I can see them working out at the gym
in their tiny leopard leotards, their muscly words
glazed with sweat. They are bench pressing
heavy symbolism. Heaving stacks of similes,
wide-stanced and grimacing. Some try so hard,
though it's a lost cause. Their wrinkled syntax,
no matter how many reps they do, will sag.
But doggedly, they jog in iambic pentameter,
Walkmans bouncing. Some glisten with clever
enjambments, end rhymes tight as green plums.
Others practice caesuras in old sweats.
But they're all there, huffing and puffing,
trying their best. Even the babies, the tender
first-drafts, struggling just to turn over, whimpering
in frustration. None of them give up.
Not the short squat little haikus
or the alexandrines trailing their long, graceful
Isadora Duncan lines. While I fidget
by the mailbox, they sail off in paper airplanes,
brave as kindergartners boarding the school bus.
They're undaunted in their innocent conviction,
their heartbreaking hope. They want to lift cars
off pinned children, rescue lost and frozen
wanderers—they'd bound out,
little whiskey barrels strapped to their necks.
They dream of shrugging off their satin
warm-up robes and wrestling with evil.

They'd hoist the sack of ordinary days
and bear it aloft like a crown. They believe
they're needed. Even at night when I sleep
and it looks like they're sleeping, they're still
at it, lying silently on the white page,
doing isometrics in the dark.

Why People Murder

I found out why people murder
in the kitchen of our house in Boulder Creek
where we'd made soybean patties,
dozens of soybean patties
ground up in our Vitamix blender and stacked,
in Saran Wrap, in the freezer.

He was in the living room.
In navy blue sweat pants and sheepskin slippers
and his pipe—he was tamping tobacco
with his thumb and looking for matches.

I picked up the knife we'd used to chop onions—
onions and carrots and whatever else it was
we put in those hopeful dry little cakes.

The details of this particular fight
are lost. But trust me, they don't matter.
Just imagine need, primitive, a baby screaming
for the tit; lust, the clawing
into another, wanting to part the other like water,
and be taken in.

And desperation, that's the big one.
You're shaky as a junkie, the pain
hums, an electric current.
You're frozen to it, a dog who's
gnawed on a cord and must be kicked off.
Save me. I'm frantic. I'm on my knees, prostrate.
I'm flat as wax across the linoleum floor.

The knife is clean. I washed it after the onions.
I lurch into the living room. My breath

comes out visible, like in cold weather.
When he sees me, he's startled, doesn't
know if he should be scared.
I'm emanating like a rod of uranium.
He says my name, tentative. I look down
at the knife, as if I were carrying it to the drawer
and took a wrong turn.

Phone Therapy

I was relief, once, for a doctor on vacation
and got a call from a man on a window sill.
This was New York, a dozen stories up.
He was going to kill himself, he said.
I said everything I could think of.
And when nothing worked, when the guy
was still determined to slide out that window
and smash his delicate skull
on the indifferent sidewalk, "Do you think,"
I asked, "you could just postpone it
until Monday, when Dr. Lewis gets back?"

The cord that connected us—strung
under the dirty streets, the pizza parlors, taxis,
women in sneakers carrying their high heels,
drunks lying in piss—that thick coiled wire
waited for the waves of sound.

In the silence I could feel the air slip
in and out of his lungs and the moment
when the motion reversed, like a goldfish
making the turn at the glass end of its tank.
I matched my breath to his, slid
into the water and swam with him.
"Okay," he agreed.

Bearing Witness

for Jacki B.

If you have lived it, then
it seems I must hear it.
—Holly Near

When the long-fingered leaves of the sycamore
flutter in the wind, spiky
seed balls swinging, and a child throws his aqua
lunch bag over the school yard railing, the last thing,
the very last thing you want to think about
is what happens to children when they're crushed
like grain in the worn mortar of the cruel.

We weep at tragedy, a baby sailing
through the windshield like a cabbage, a shoe.
The young remnants of war, arms sheared and eyeless,
they lie like eggs on the rescue center's bare floor.

But we draw a line at the sadistic,
as if our yellow plastic tape would keep harm
confined. We don't want to know
what generations of terror do to the young
who are fed like cloth
under the machine's relentless needle.

In the paper, we'll read about the ordinary neighbor
who chopped up boys; at the movies we pay
to shoot up that adrenaline rush—
and the spent aftermath, relief
like a long-awaited piss.

But face to face with the living prey,
we turn away, rev the motor, as though
we've seen a ghost—which, in a way, we have:
one who wanders the world,
tugging on sleeves, trying to find the road home.

And if we stop, all our fears
will come to pass. The knowledge of evil
will coat us like grease
from a long shift at the griddle. Our sweat
will smell like the sweat of the victims.

And this is why you do it—listen
at the outskirts of what our species
has accomplished, listen until the world is flat
again, and you are standing on its edge.
This is why you hold them in your arms, allowing
their snot to smear your skin, their sour
breath to mist your face. You listen
to slash the membrane that divides us, to plant
the hard shiny seed of yourself
in the common earth. You crank
open the rusty hinge of your heart
like an old beach umbrella. Because God
is not a flash of diamond light. God is
the kicked child, the child
who rocks alone in the basement,
the one fucked so many times
she does not know her name, her mind
burning like a star.

The Thing Is

to love life, to love it even
when you have no stomach for it
and everything you've held dear
crumbles like burnt paper in your hands,
your throat filled with the silt of it.
When grief sits with you, its tropical heat
thickening the air, heavy as water
more fit for gills than lungs;
when grief weights you like your own flesh
only more of it, an obesity of grief,
you think, *How can a body withstand this?*
Then you hold life like a face
between your palms, a plain face,
no charming smile, no violet eyes,
and you say, yes, I will take you
I will love you, again.

Sleeping Next to the Man on the Plane

I'm not well. Neither is he.
Periodically he pulls out a handkerchief
and blows his nose. I worry
about germs, but appreciate how he shares
the armrest—especially
considering his size—too large
to lay the tray over his lap.
His seatbelt barely buckles. At least
he doesn't have to ask for an extender
for which I imagine him grateful. Our upper arms
press against each other, like apricots growing
from the same node. My arm is warm
where his touches it. I close my eyes.
In the chilly, oxygen-poor air, I am glad
to be close to his breathing mass.
We want our own species. We want
to lie down next to our own kind.
Even here in this metal encumbrance, hurtling
improbably 30,000 feet above the earth,
with all this civilization—down
to the chicken-or-lasagna in their
environmentally-incorrect packets,
even as the woman behind me is swiping
her credit card on the phone embedded
in my headrest and the folks in first
are watching their individual movies
on personal screens, I lean
into this stranger, seeking primitive comfort—
heat, touch, breath—as we slip
into the ancient vulnerability of sleep.

I Love the Way Men Crack

I love the way men crack
open when their wives leave them,
their sheaths curling back like the split
shells of roasted chestnuts, exposing
the sweet creamy meat. They call you
and unburden their hearts the way a woman
takes off her jewels, the heavy
pendant earrings, the stiff lace gown and corset,
and slips into a loose kimono.
It's like you've both had a couple shots
of really good scotch and snow is falling
in the cone of light under the street lamp—
large slow flakes that float down in the opalescent glow.

They tell you all the pain pressed into their chests,
their disappointed penises, their empty hands.
As they sift through the betrayals and regrets,
their shocked realization of how hard they tried,
the way they shouldered the yoke
with such stupid good faith,
they grow younger and younger. They cry
with the unselfconsciousness of children.
When they hug you, they cling.
Like someone who's needed glasses for a long time—
and finally got them—they look around
just for the pleasure of it: the detail,
the sharp edges of what the world has to offer.

And when they fall in love again, it only gets better.
Their hearts are stuffed full as eclairs
and the custard oozes out at a touch.
They love her, they love you, they love everyone.
They drag out all the musty sorrows and joys

from the basement where they've been shoved
with mitts and coin collections. They tell you
things they've never told anyone.
Fresh from loving her, they come glowing
like souls slipping into the bodies
of babies about to be born.

Then a year goes by. Or two.
Like broken bones, they knit back together.
They grow like grass and bushes and trees
after a forest fire, covering the seared earth.

Getting My Hands on My Mother's Body

I go to my mother in the hospital
like a child on the first day of school.
I watch for my stop on the train,
my small bag of books on my lap.

And she is alive there. Pale
and mottled as the underside of flounder.
Her eyes are closed, and as I get closer
I see tiny white flakes at the roots
of her sparse lashes, like bits of shell
at the shoreline. Her body rises
and falls like a calm ocean.
"Have you eaten?" she asks.

My tasks are so simple, I master them at once.
The ice machine, the hot water dispenser,
the apartment-size refrigerator with three kinds of juice.
After the bedpan, I wet a washcloth
and she wipes each finger delicately.

In the afternoon, I knit.
If she's feeling up to it, she tells me stories.
How Harry used to save his candy,
then taunt her as he nibbled each
microscopic, languorous bite.
And in high school, in an aberration of bravado,
she wrote *Love 'Em and Leave 'Em*
on the back of her yellow slicker
and had to wear it all four years.

Today I cut her toenails.
It's a delicate job. A nick
could mean gangrene.

As a child, I'd begged for this.
She let me fix her up with mascara and rouge,
but drew the line at toes.
"Cut my hair," she'd say, "I need my feet to work."
I position the clipper precisely
at each thick nail, yellowed as old ivory.
There is no talking now. I concentrate
as though I'm cutting the facets of the Hope Diamond.

Afterward, she lets me smooth
lotion into her lumpy feet. About massage,
she always said, "I don't want anyone mauling me."
But this once, like a woman who's refused
a suitor so many times he's given up hope,
she relents, and I rub the old arches,
the callused heels, circle knobby ankle bones
and slip my fingers gently between the toes
with which she's entrusted me.

I think there must be something more to say.
But she's already told me she's not afraid
to die. And the rest, even I know, is obvious.

While she sleeps, I read
A Brief History of Time. I don't entirely
understand how the twins are different ages
when one returns from her voyage
at the speed of light. But I've got redshift
and the Doppler effect down cold
and it's tranquil now
to read Hawking's patient discussion
about whether the universe is expanding,
contracting, or staying the same.

And What If I Spoke of Despair

And what if I spoke of despair—who doesn't
feel it? Who doesn't know the way it seizes,
leaving us limp, deafened by the slosh
of our own blood, rushing
through the narrow, personal
channels of grief. It's beauty
that brings it on, calls it out from the wings
for one more song. Rain
pooled on a fallen oak leaf, reflecting
the pale cloudy sky, dark canopy
of foliage not yet fallen. Or the red moon
in September, so large you have to pull over
at the top of Bayona and stare, like a photo
of a lover in his uniform, not yet gone;
or your own self, as a child,
on that day your family stayed
at the sea, watching the sun drift down,
lazy as a beach ball, and you fell asleep with sand
in the crack of your smooth behind.
That's when you can't deny it. Water. Air.
They're still here, like a mother's palms,
sweeping hair off our brow, her scent
swirling around us. But now your own
car is pumping poison, delivering its fair
share of destruction. We've created a salmon
with the red, white, and blue shining on one side.
Frog genes spliced into tomatoes—as if
the tomato hasn't been humiliated enough.
I heard a man argue that genetic
engineering was more dangerous
than a nuclear bomb. Should I be thankful
he was alarmed by one threat, or worried
he'd gotten used to the other? Maybe I can't

offer you any more than you can offer me—
but what if I stopped on the trail, with shreds
of manzanita bark lying in russet scrolls
and yellow bay leaves, little lanterns
in the dim afternoon, and cradled despair
in my arms, the way I held my own babies
after they'd fallen asleep, when there was no
reason to hold them, only
I didn't want to put them down.

Insomnia

All over the world, people can't sleep.
In different time zones, they are lying awake,
bodies still, minds trudging along like child laborers.

They worry about bills. They worry
whether the shoes they just bought
are really too small. One's husband died,
her son left for college, and she doesn't
know how to program the VCR.

Another was beaten by her husband.
One is planning a getaway.
One holding stolen goods.

One's on the plaid couch in ICU. His daughter,
it turned out, actually does have a brain tumor
even though the doctor said they'd do the MRI just
to rule it out. The woman on the other couch
is snoring—which is strangely soothing—
evidence that people do sleep.

Some are lying on Charisma sheets.
Some in hammocks. Some in jail. Some
under bridges. One is at the North Pole
studying the impact of pollution.

A man in Massachusetts thinks about a lover
he once had in Dar es Salaam and the jasmine
blossoms she strung along the shaft of a silver
pin, fastened in her hair at night. Coincidentally,
the lover, now in Rome, remembers
looking out the window over the sink
when she was washing dishes. He was reading

in a lawn chair and she thought how,
perhaps for the first time, she wasn't lonely.

Some are too cold. Some
too hot. Some hungry. Some in pain.
Some are in hotels listening to people having sex
in the next room. Some are crying.
One the cat woke up
and now she's worried about the rash
she noticed in the evening and wonders
if her daughter, who's afraid to swim,
should be pushed.

Some get up. Others stay in bed.
They eat Oreo's or drink wine—or both.
Many read. A few make intricate
Halloween costumes: a peacock
with eight real feathers in the tail.
Some check their e-mail. They try
sleep tapes, hypnosis, drugs.
And listen to their clocks tick, smartly
as women in high heels.

Those who can, cling to their mates,
an ear pressed to those neighboring lungs like a
stethoscope, hoping to catch a ride
on the steady sleep breath of the other, to be carried
like a seed on the body of the one who is able.

Right now, in Japan, dawn is coming
and everyone who's been up all night
is relieved. They can stop trying.
In Guatemala, though, the insomniacs are just
getting started and have the whole
night ahead of them. It's like a wave
at the baseball stadium, hands
around the world.

So here's a prayer
for the wakeful, the souls who can't rest:
As you lie with eyes
open or closed, may something
comfort you—a mockingbird, a breeze, the smell
of crushed mint, Chopin's Nocturnes,
your child's birth, a kiss,
or even me—in my chilly kitchen
with my coat over my nightgown—thinking of you.

Notes

"Pay for It," p. 25: Robert Bly, *Iron John* (New York: Addison-Wesley, 1990) p. 176.

"If There Is No God," p. 29: Lyrics by Dorothy Fields; music by Jimmy McHugh.

Acknowledgments

Grateful acknowledgment is made to the editors of the following publications in which these works or earlier versions of them previously appeared:

Alaska Quarterly Review: "Why People Murder";
The Beloit Poetry Journal: "I Love the Way Men Crack";
Bridges: "Guilt";
Comstock Review: "Tigers and People";
DoubleTake: "Jack Gottlieb's in Love";
Field: "God and the G-Spot," "His Teeth";
The Greensboro Review: "Marriage Without Sex," "Pay for It";
Kalliope: "Birds Do It," "Everything on the Menu";
Mangrove: "Poem to My Sex at Fifty-One";
The Missouri Review: "And What If I Spoke of Despair";
Nimrod: "Can't Get Over Her," "Mighty Strong Poems," "Phone Therapy";
The Paterson Literary Review: "Backdoor Karaoke," "If," "Sleeping Next to the Man on the Plane";
Porter Gulch Review: "Laundry";
Piedmont Literary Review: "In My Hands";
Quarry West: "Sometimes, After Making Love";
Red Rock: "The Moon";
Sojourner: "Getting My Hands on My Mother's Body," "The Sad Truth," "Working in the Garden";
The Sun: "Worry";
Tribes: "Remodeling the Bathroom";
Women's Studies Quarterly: "If There Is No God";
ZYZZYVA: "Tulip Blossoms."

"Bearing Witness" appears in *Like Thunder: Poets Respond to Violence in America* (University of Iowa Press); "Sometimes, After Making Love" appears in *Intimate Kisses: The Poetry of Sexual Pleasure* (New World Library); "For My Daughter on Her Twenty-First Birthday" appears as

"Mules of Love" in *Baby Blessings: Prayers and Poems Celebrating Mothers and Babies* (Harmony Books); "The Thing Is" appears in *Bedside Prayers* (HarperCollins), *Bless the Day* (Kodansha), and *Prayers for a Thousand Years* (HarperSan Francisco); "After Our Daughter's Wedding" and "God and the G-Spot" appear in *Women Artists Datebook* (Syracuse Cultural Workers).

"Can't Get Over Her," "Mighty Strong Poems," and "Phone Therapy" were selected for the 2000 Pablo Neruda Prize from *Nimrod/Hardman*.

"And What If I Spoke of Despair" was selected for the 2002 Larry Levis Editor's Prize for Poetry from *The Missouri Review*.

My sincere gratitude to all my students, teachers, and friends, with special thanks to Florence Howe, Lucy Diggs, Michael Ponsor, and Charlotte Raymond for early and continuing support; to Sharon Olds for the right words at the right time; to Kim Addonizio, Joe Millar, and Thom Ward for generous and insightful critique; and most of all, to Dorianne Laux, without whom my poems would still be in their pajamas, sipping coffee, trying to wake up.

About the Author

Ellen Bass co-edited the groundbreaking book, *No More Masks!: An Anthology of Poems by Women* and has published four previous volumes of poetry, *I'm Not Your Laughing Daughter*, *Of Separateness and Merging*, *For Earthly Survival*, and *Our Stunning Harvest*. Her nonfiction books include *I Never Told Anyone*, *Free Your Mind*, and *The Courage to Heal*, which has been translated into nine languages. Among her awards are the Elliston Book Award from the University of Cincinnati, The Pablo Neruda Prize from *Nimrod/Hardman*, and the Larry Levis Editor's Prize from *The Missouri Review*. She lives in Santa Cruz, CA, where she has taught creative writing since 1974.

BOA EDITIONS, LTD.

AMERICAN POETS CONTINUUM SERIES

No. 1   *The Fuhrer Bunker: A Cycle of Poems in Progress*
W. D. Snodgrass

No. 2   *She*
M. L. Rosenthal

No. 3   *Living With Distance*
Ralph J. Mills, Jr.

No. 4   *Not Just Any Death*
Michael Waters

No. 5   *That Was Then: New and Selected Poems*
Isabella Gardner

No. 6   *Things That Happen Where There Aren't Any People*
William Stafford

No. 7   *The Bridge of Change: Poems 1974–1980*
John Logan

No. 8   *Signatures*
Joseph Stroud

No. 9   *People Live Here: Selected Poems 1949–1983*
Louis Simpson

No. 10   *Yin*
Carolyn Kizer

No. 11   *Duhamel: Ideas of Order in Little Canada*
Bill Tremblay

No. 12   *Seeing It Was So*
Anthony Piccione

No. 13   *Hyam Plutzik: The Collected Poems*

No. 14   *Good Woman: Poems and a Memoir 1969–1980*
Lucille Clifton

No. 15   *Next: New Poems*
Lucille Clifton

No. 16   *Roxa: Voices of the Culver Family*
William B. Patrick

No. 17   *John Logan: The Collected Poems*

No. 18   *Isabella Gardner: The Collected Poems*

No. 19   *The Sunken Lightship*
Peter Makuck

No. 20   *The City in Which I Love You*
Li-Young Lee

No. 21   *Quilting: Poems 1987–1990*
Lucille Clifton

No. 22   *John Logan: The Collected Fiction*

No. 23   *Shenandoah and Other Verse Plays*
Delmore Schwartz

No. 24   *Nobody Lives on Arthur Godfrey Boulevard*
Gerald Costanzo

No. 25   *The Book of Names: New and Selected Poems*
Barton Sutter

No. 26   *Each in His Season*
W. D. Snodgrass

No. 27   *Wordworks: Poems Selected and New*
Richard Kostelanetz

No. 28   *What We Carry*
Dorianne Laux

No. 29   *Red Suitcase*
Naomi Shihab Nye

No. 30   *Song*
Brigit Pegeen Kelly

No. 31   *The Fuehrer Bunker: The Complete Cycle*
W. D. Snodgrass

No. 32   *For the Kingdom*
Anthony Piccione

No. 33   *The Quicken Tree*
Bill Knott

No. 34   *These Upraised Hands*
William B. Patrick

No. 35   *Crazy Horse in Stillness*
William Heyen

No. 36   *Quick, Now, Always*
Mark Irwin

Colophon

The publication of *Mules of Love*
was made possible by the special support
of the following individuals:

Rochelle & Herbert Bass
Elise Collins-Shields
Shirley & Chip Dawson
Jill Dyche
Dr. Henry & Beverly French
Dane & Judy Gordon
Kip & Deb Hale
Robert & Willy Hursh
Dorothy & Henry Hwang
Kathryn Kaufman
Dr. Leo & Charlotte Landhuis
Boo Poulin
Deborah Ronnen
Annette & Aaron Satloff
Jane Schuster
Thomas R. Ward
Pat & Michael Wilder

This book was typeset in Goudy
with Adobe Woodtype Ornaments
by Richard Foerster, York Beach, Maine.
Cover design is by Daphne Poulin-Stofer.
The cover painting, *Mules of Love*, is by Beverly Sky,
courtesy of the artist. Printing was by
McNaughton & Gunn, Saline, Michigan.